KU-100-392

Burning Whins
and other poems

LIZ NIVEN

Luath Press Limited

EDINBURGH

www.luath.co.uk

ABERDEENSHIRE LIBRARY AND INFORMATION SERVICES	
1726097	
HJ	437966
821 NIV	£8.99
SC	EXAS

First Published 2004

The author's right to be identified as author of this book under the
Copyright, Designer and Patents Acts 1988 has been asserted.

The publisher acknowledges subsidy from

 Scottish Arts Council

towards the publication of this book.

The paper used in this book is recyclable. It is made from low
chlorine pulps produced in a low energy, low emission manner
from renewable forests.

Lino cuts by Hugh Bryden

Printed and bound by
DigiSource (GB), Livingston

Typeset in Sabon 10.5 by
S Fairgrieve, Edinburgh 0131 658 1763

© Liz Niven

For John, David, Andrew & Jenny

Acknowledgements

I would like to acknowledge the support of a Scottish Arts Council Writers' Bursary in the course of writing this book.

I would like to thank Caroline Storey, Sheena Mitchell and Callum Smith at Inverness Airport for all their assistance and kindness back at 'base'. Also, to Bjorn Sandison, the young pilot from Shetland who managed to make me feel at home high in the sky above Scotland.

As always to my family and friends who make me feel at home on the ground and who keep my feet there while ma heid's in the clouds 'including poet-friends Janet Paisley and Ron Butlin'.

Some of these poems have appeared in the following journals and anthologies:

Chapman, Gaelforce, Flights with Attitude, New Writing Scotland 19 (ASLS), *Markings, Nerve, Poetry Scotland, Deliberately Thirsty, Lallans, Gairfish, Mr Burns for Supper, Modern Scottish Women Poets* (Canongate), *Edinburgh: an Intimate City, Lallans, Ars Poetica: Slovakia*, Canada, *Words Without Borders*, NY, USA. Some have been broadcast on BBC Radio Scotland, BBC Ulster and ITV television.

Contents

SECTION I

An Turas: The Journey or The Angels' Share

The poems in this section were commissioned by the Highlands and Islands Ltd, as part of their Gateway Arts Project. Nine destinations were flown to from Inverness and Glasgow Airport and these narrative poems tell the story of the journeys.

This section is dedicated to all the wonderful Islanders who welcomed me on my travels.

Something for the weekend, Madam?
(Inverness)

The Duty manager looks tired.
Five o clock and she's
just started nightshift.

Saturday night at eleven
before she'll be home.
Holidaymakers just settling
into foreign lands,
others home to the bosom
of family.

What's the strangest thing
you've found left
on an aeroplane? I ask.

She points out a tray
of mobile phones,
two black leather
horse whips,
tells us of the
brass vibrator,
nine inches long,
stuffed down the men's toilet.

Oddly enough, it's
long since vanished.

On my next plane,
I eye the cabin crew
with suspicion,
notice their wide
lipstick smiles.

Traffic Control Tower

outside the three hundred and sixty degree window
a brown blur of kestrel   hovers
black wagtails peer in while
rabbits, hare, examine the deer fence

inside, traffic control men watch,
                    heads bobbing like pert birds
fielding calls from incoming, outgoing planes
RAF Lossiemouth, the local flying club,
half hour weather reports to Bracknell

an unexpected Nature reserve
when pregnant badgers seeking warmth
gathered round the electric transformer
protected species not moved till
baby cubs were born

skeins of migratory geese
                    scatter   at the red van's siren
of imitation birds distress call
once, a flock blew up an engine,
another ingested in a plane

among the confusion of dials, graphs, faxes
sits a collection of tiny models –
gifts from the Danish Legoland plane

and jargon –
tear drop, arc, no visuals,
                    altered flight paths on a stormy day
bring their own language

zulu time or UTC
the universe shares time zones here
logic breaking barriers

the tower sways in a sudden gale
          birds   trees   slant off into horizons
suspended between soil and sky
this bubble buzzes its high tec static
bursts   into action as a silver dot   appears
through cloud
announcing arrival
words or traffic, all striving, in our own ways
to put order over possible chaos.

Inverness Airport

A day in the life of...

The foyer empties and fills like a tidal wash in nearby Ness.
Arrivals are mostly brisk, happy,
departures linger, drawn out affairs.

A young couple practically devour each other.
A dog is stroked till its eyes roll upward.

A small boy has read an entire book
about elk, moose, American deer,
and wants to prove it.

The Avis Hire lady politely
listens to a red-faced man,
demanding a car.

Security calmly checks in
bikes, cats, surf boards
the size of dolphins

The Airport shop lady dispenses
ten cigarettes and a box of matches.
Real smokers buy twenty and a lighter.
She knows the nervous.

Late planes at Luton,
technical failures at Faro,
a butterfly flapping its wings in the forest,
Ground Staff explain cause and effect.

Café Rapide slows, sells
coffee, tea, words of condolence.

The Airport Chapel book fills:

Beautiful, red-stained glass cross,
scent of potpourri

We brought you home to Skye
Always in our hearts

Some other smell than antiseptic

The passing of the Queen Mother

My heart's broken as my son hasn't spoken to me,
Since my remarriage seven years ago

bedside to airside, cross-section of travellers' prayers.

The last flights are in, gone out.
Calm descends but for
the Pristine Cleaner's hoover
singing a high-pitched sound,
after sucking up some small, green, metallic hearts.

Somebody has fallen in love, married, gone on honeymoon,
while these little hearts have fallen out.

The airport cat, if there was one,
would be put out for the night,
the twenty four hour clocks wound up.

Staff, team spirit high, chatter,
check tomorrow's rota,
choose an Inverness pub.

Inverness to Stornoway

Frost
over Ardesier
October morning
fine icing sugar
dusting
the bens
a world still
wakening
white voids ahead
visible through
the open cockpit door

I'm being delivered
with the papers
on the Stornoway flight
Highland Airways
four seats for folk
sixteen for newspapers
wrapped in their
grey sleeping bags

we are in the minority here
all this print
might weigh me down
so many words to choose from

The Learning Shop
(Stornoway)

Bused, taxied, flown in from
Stornoway, Leverburgh, Benbecula,
we're in the Airport Business Room
having a workshop.

Skills taken for granted are cherished, developed.
Not everyone finds writing easy,
never mind making poems.
Yet here we're all creating, composing, trying.

Through a picture landscape window,
all sky and cloud, planes land, leave,
passengers and staff dart, tarmac shines.

We work on till an urn of soup is delivered,
October sun blends with morning rain,
produces yet another Highland rainbow.

Chat can happen now.

Paul proposed to his wife in Belfast's Botanic Gardens;
Janet hasn't washed her hair because of another island powercut;
Young Frankie dreams of Russia;
Claire from England loves Harris.

Marie-Anne, sixteen year old eyes shining,
hopes for work here, near home.
With us too is her mother, grandmother,
three generations, at the Island's *Learning Shop.*

The quiet man, who says he has no poetry, tells me,
I live on the road to the Callanish Stones,

We eat, drink, laugh together,
discover little pots of gold,
are where you least expect them.

An Turas: The Journey
(Tiree)

Six fifty Glasgow train
to the airport, damp dark
Monday morning blueness.

Building sites, cranes,
iron poles jut into landscapes,
foundations hole horizons.

At Gateway Two, a teacher from Tiree,
red travel-sickness wristbands, introduces herself.
A lady butcher from Islay waits too.

I discover the school technician's mother
lives next door to mine in Glasgow,
roots and webs never far in this wee land.

The Art teacher's camera captures my arrival.
A common island phenomena, he's multi-hatted and we're off
to the High School, where pupils write of journeys:

Buying playing cards to while away the time,
seeing Harold and wee Duncan loading
a trailer, the smell of diesel.

The Art teacher's son drives me
to the Glassary Guest House,
moon glistening over water.

A dry stane dyker,
but in his van sleeps a surf board.
Tiree is the 'Hawaii of the North'.

Modern legends of the *Wave Classic*
sit side by side with Ancient tales:
The Ringing Stane will sink the island if it breaks

When Kennesmuir sank off Balevulin,
a cargo of magenta dye
changed the island's fashion colours.

And now, the latest talking point,
the Folly of *An Turas.*
At Gott Bay pier, a white wall leads us over

slatted wooden boards, under beamed ceilings,
to the glass box enclosure
        breaking through a stone wall dyke.

Above our heads, rain water, sand swirl.
Through this looking-glass a wonderland world;
redshanks wade over liquid pools,

sheep nibble machair knapweed,
a lapwing takes off like a small Cessna,
cries across the isle as Atlantic breakers beckon.

Travellers' traces live on in salt-tanged tongues;
Norse in *pols, baghs*.
Gaelic at *Feis Thiriodh* celebrations.

Words birl your head when you wake
to the sound of wind and corncrake,
on this *Isle beneath the sea*.

Through centuries, city or sand, journeys shift foundations,
rebuild lines to sift through for solid ground.

Gateway 2
(Glasgow)

for Aimara

Erra Barra plane.
Erra its perra propellers.
Utterly amazing.
Twin otter,
Lands oan a beach.
Cannae believe it?
Tide's in, doesnae land.
Naw, A'm no taking ye fir a ride.
S'true.
S' real, man.

Barra Airport

On arrival customers are given a questionnaire:

Dear Customer,
This is your opportunity to tell us,
Highland and Islands Airports
About the kind of service provided for you.
Please fill in the form
Place it in the sealed box provided
The questionnaire is <u>confidential.</u>

Boxes give choices of:
Good   Average   Poor

We can comment upon:
The seating arrangements in the Terminal Building
The toilets, including standard of disabled toilets
The café
The car park
Passenger service (Loganair)

Then we are invited to tell of *any suggestions, difficulties you
may have experienced, or comments on the above.*

We can continue on the other side if necessary.

the other side takes on
a new meaning, I must have been good in another life
for this one I'm now in has brought me to Barra.

So, where to begin this form filling?

This tiny *De Havilland Twin Otter*
has touched down on a beach.

A pebble-smooth landing
onto beige, soft sand.
Grains trail the center aisle,
a tractor greets us for our luggage.

We have no desire to comment on
seats, toilets, cafés or car park.

We just want to tell about the Barra flight;
       low level height which lets you
       track land formations beneath
       water-linked peninsulas,
       bird-like landing onto soft surface,
       spray spattering the windows,
       sun rays pink, orange as a goose leg,
       a cemetery's headstones like Lewis chessmen.

And inland what treaures awaited:
a taxi driver without a voice–box
presses a small throat valve to let him talk.

And this island sure could take your breath away.
He has stories galore, as he drives me round past
the *Star of the Sea* overlooking the land,
to Castlebay, where Kisimuil Castle,
seat of the Clan MacNeil, defies gravity and

floats.

A palm tree, courtesy of the warm Gulf winds,
holds out its open-hand welcome,
silhouetted against the sky.

I speak to Cara, Louise, Megan and Amy,
writing their poems in Barra High School,
Vatersay night, sleeping sea, our calm world.

An airport fanatic in the Guest House
is in love, too, with the Barra flight.

And a tall man from a London Alms House
cycling round the Hebrides.

Mrs McIntosh of the Kisimuil Galley,
leaves me, a stranger, to mind the shop
while she dashes home for a CDRom.

At the village Post Office,
a silversmith sends his work,
apologising for such parcels,
It's the time of year, he tells Moira and Morag.
Knightsbridge is selling 'Gaeltime'.

Back at the Airport, a painted wall hanging;
Barra Air Service
It's our lifeline
By Eoligarry Primary School
We know it's that and more.

Boarding again,
the tractor loads bags onto
sand-sprinkled aisles.
A London journalist flies too,
wondering which words
to tell a city of tide dictated take-offs.

Another golden sun,
the windows spraying lightly,
not a trace of wind moves the *machair.*
I've forgotten to fill in the form.
We all have.

Any Comments?
Beware, the Barra flight can enter your soul,
leave part of your heart like driftwood,
on a Hebridean shore.

Benbecula Beasts

In the pick up bus to Glasgow Airport,
American tourists are heading home.
One holds a thin stream of ticket tape,
white as a winding island road.

Here, she shouts to her guy across the aisle.
Put that in your scrapbook.
It'll be a sort of border.
Cool, he says. *Swing down, sister.*

At Departures a small cat in a box
checks in, miaouwing furiously.
Tog Ort gu Siar/Hop on the Western Line
A poster says.

Inverness to Stornoway,
Benbecula, then Barra.

Dinner time at the Firefighters Office, rabbit curry again.
Lapwings, starlings litter the runaway, obstruct planes.
Migratory geese scare more easily,
seasonal visitors who know their place.

A Firefighter offers to show me the Island,
Grimsay, views of the Uists,
the Lewes College Museum where pictures show
the old bridge before the Causeway,

its concrete pillars triangular span.
Now, the land has no sea borders,
cars and more can cross with ease,
signs warn of otters crossing roads.

This to-ing and fro-ing over land, sea, sky
how easily now we move, in and out
of each other's space, across
islands, cities, countries, continents.

In the distance, Military Base houses
remind us times are not always harmonious.
Boundaries can be bridged or breached.

The Angels' Share
(Islay)

Once again, true to form at every Airport I've been,
the Firefighters are a real team and so kind.
Have our car, they urge, *see the Island.*
First though, you must come on our daily check.

Alarmingly, I'm ushered onto a fire engine;
A massive dragon beast.
We tear down the tarmac like devils.

Being a sea-edged runway, crew have
lifeboats, Land Rovers, sea-going expertise.
But it's me that's all at sea, when they say I should drive.

On with the hard hat in canary yellow
(appropriate colour to match my cowardice)
and we're off again sirens blowing.

The runway's white arrow
points us skyward, we might lift off at any moment
I imagine fleetingly a flying fire engine.

It could become a famous fable for Islay,
replace tales of Loch Finlaggan,
seat of the Lords of the Isles,
or the famous Feis for Gaelic music.

Nights round the fire folk would tell,
of the day in November,
when the Islay Firefighters took off.

Sheep eyeball us curiously as we mount the grass.
I'm told to keep going off the tarmac onto the field.
We must practice rescues at the water's edge.

I feel the vehicle lurch to
forty five degrees, my heart goes with it.
A couple of startled rabbits follow.

Best not look in the wing mirrors.
Of course, I do. Red painted sides stretch for miles.
I'm driving a giant.

Later, the HIAL borrowed car feels like a midget
as I take off round this green haven,
a whisky lover's paradise.

Pass names of villages I've only
ever seen on bottles;
Caol Ila, Bunnahabhainn,
Lagavulin, Bruichladdich

An ex-exciseman recounts his working days.
Tomorrow I'll check the cradle roll,
in Bowmore's round church,
for a friend who was born here.

Legend has it that, unlike our memories,
no corners are there for the Devil to hide in.

That night in Bowmore, I listen to locals,
incomers (seventeen years, mind you).
The American Vietnamese Pilot,
who's bought the Laird's old house.

Tourists doing the distilleries.
A dark-haired girl who sits on a bar stool
drinking her way through many malts,
jotting notes as she does,
the print swaying from side to side.

It can be hard to pin words down,
not lose something,
in such circumstances.

Across the island, casks sleep
ten, twelve, twenty years,
till daylight-kissed they wake,
distilled to perfection.

Rapid processing of memories
might prove more elusive
for print or poetry;
maturing my journey
into something labelled poem.

*Note: The Angels' Share is the amount of whisky lost in evaporation during
distillation.*

Wick

Small one-syllable town;
no-one could hold a candle to you
in the herring days,

women walking the miles
to markets down coast.

Or, in the hey days of oil,
men leaving for rigs, prospects of wealth
gleaming their eyes.

Here, it's all Norse words mixed in the Scots.
Staxigoe and Papigoe,

and the b&b lady, pure Caithness,
tells me of her *dowgs* and horses on the *fairm;*
the language clashing against the Gaelic,

running, like Lewisian gneiss
through the rest of this land.

Now, arcing out to Orkney
in this small Cessna plane,
harbour waters boiling below,

your lights fade
though the faces of your young

remain clear, ready to take off,
spread their own wings, leave the Flow country,
as the snow gates close at the Burriehead Brae.

2 Orkney poems

1. Orkneyinga Saga: Far from Home

Fara
Honda
Flotta
Swona
Stroma
Balfour
Toab

Deerness
Westness
Stromnness
Westray
Rousay
Stronsay
Aith

Ronaldsay
Melsetter
Copinsay
Shapinsay
Wasbister
Otters wick

Holm.

2. The Young Man of Hoy said to his Old Man

Hey, Dad,

You'd get stacks of street cred
if you'd do as I say.

Façade retention is the latest thing.

You could become an
eighty feet high
top class restaurant.

Kit out your interior with
high tec steel, tubular chrome,
be an ultra-modern superstructure of
combined and compressed
melamine filaments of
polyurethane PVC.
A towering lookout over the
North Sea, Pentland Firth and
from the top 16th floor, the
Irish Sea, maybe.

You could serve up a stushie
with your fresh organic sushie
local fish, sun-dried veg.

It would go down a storm up here,
with wind surfers.

How about a glass-topped dome
looking out to the sky?

Birds, gannets, seals,
maybe a dolphin or two.
Imagine the sunsets,
the Aurora Borealis,
light not fading all summer,
the clear pure air.

Come on Old Man, why
have you nothing to say?

Shetland Journey

Seven in the morning at the Airport foyer.
A young pilot takes my bag.

I'm Bjorn, he tells me.
We cross the tarmac.

Once, policemen looked young, now it's pilots.
I'll call him Bjorn, the baby pilot.

Would you like to climb in?
Over the wing or over the newspapers?

Climb to where? I ask, then see there are no seats,
except in the cockpit. My worst fears are realized.

I climb over *Daily Mails, Expresses,*
The sun is starting to rise in the East.

If I sink low enough in my chair,
I won't see over the black range of dials before me,

won't see the nose of the plane, runway ahead.
The propellers rotate, left, then right.

I ask Bjorn, aren't there usually two pilots?
Even the wee Stornoway mail plane had two.

No, he says, *after seven hundred flying hours,*
we can go solo.

How many hours have you? I ask
Seven hundred, he smiles, *my first solo today.*

I'm speechless for a while, remember my
first car ride after passing my driving test.

We move through clouds
thick and static, thin and swift.

Somebody must have as many words for clouds
as Eskimos have for snow.

The sun bursts through the horizon on my right.
Red and pink streaks flash like aluminium flares.

There's a glare from the sky and we're in it.
This is a whole new world up here.

Bjorn points out Fair Isle below,
Sumburgh Head, and the Airport,

is high tec next to Jarlshof's ancient stone.
Prehistoric, Norse, now us; it's seen it all.

Take control? Asks Bjorn. My mind loses it.
Touching the joystick, we judder

like the jelly my legs have turned into.
Now I am a bird, a cloud, an angel.

Stone, water, light, my head buzzes.
So does the airport when we land,

for it's full of oil workers heading rig wise.
There is no further north in this tiny country,

nearer Norway than Scottish mainland.
dowry land for a Danish Princess.

Most maps displace it miles south,
its voices foreign to southern lugs.

Later, I read of reduced revenues,
the campaign to invoke Udal Law,

give nothing to the Crown.
Dunna chuck bruck.

For now, the treasure's all mine,
these Northern journeys gifts

to leave one wordless.

*Udal Law is an ancient Norse system which allowed people to
own property outright without title deed or any feudal claims of
crown precedence.*

Campbeltown
The road not taken: 5 November 2003

Four pm Glasgow Airport,
a gale blowing outside.
At Departure Gate 2, passengers wait
for the Campbeltown plane.

The Ground Crew have donned
overcoats and yellow fluorescent jackets.
We're issued with letters from HIAL:
Due to adverse conditions ...

Ironic if this is cancelled.
The only flight on a mainland route,
the rest unreachable by land.
A young girl tells me she has

organized a childminder,
just in case.
She's used to such scenarios,
but others aren't.

A man tells everybody,
he has driven to Stansted,
flown to Glasgow, waited three hours,
and hopes to get to Campbeltown tonight.

One woman, just left hospital,
looks drawn and tired
We climb aboard and wait.
The Pilot assures us

he *will do his best,*
but outside the windows,
nothing is visible.
We are in a grey soup.

A young man in a white zipper jacket,
blue baseball cap, opens his duffle bag,
takes out a tabloid as turbulence shifts
the black headlines in his hands.

Surface transport will be provided
or our flights rescheduled

The plane circles Campbeltown,
turns back across the Clyde.
Ten minutes over and the sky clears,
below us the lights of Dumbarton, Glasgow

startle with their sudden sparkle.
A flash of red sprays into the air
followed by blues, purples, fluorescent greens.
Every few miles the same thing is happening.

We strain our necks to watch,
utter small gasps and sighs,
realise it's Guy Fawkes' fireworks
exploding beneath us.

The young mother stops
thinking of her baby for a few moments,
the lady out of hospital
briefly forgets her pain,

the man far travelled marvels too.
Even the youth in the baseball cap
is watching,
his paper fallen to his lap,

our bird's eye view of this city celebrating
now, with the sky cleared above us, stars reappear.
We are sandwiched between marvels
we might never have seen,

the road not taken, yielding up
its other possibilities.

SECTION II
Merrick tae Criffel

'Fae the braes o Glen App tae the brigen o Dumfries'.

Carlyle at Ecclefechan

Writing is a dreadful labour,
Yet not so dreadful as idleness,
said Thomas Carlyle with vigour,
in a rare moment of digression,
from his weighty tomes of work
of which intellectual thought formed the bulk.

Yet the domestic details are of huge importance,
the Ecclefechan cake better known,
Fourdes' fondness for Jane Carlyle quoted,
then posthumous doubts against Carlyle sown.
His French Revolution manuscript tirade
rekindled a fire by an unthinking maid.

Who knows the town of the speckled kirk,
was home to the ghosts of the intellectually quick?

Notes on John Paul Jones

Born near Kirkcudbright, then American
immigrant and notable Freemason.
Lodges across continents knew his name.
Establishing US fleets brought him fame.
Hence invited by Catherine the Great
to help Russia's army in a Turk's defeat.

'Father of the American Navy',
eighteenth century hero honoured.
Russian exploits legendary.
US Naval Academy buried.

*Though the Russian glory was short-lived when
a false charge of molesting was made, then
dropped, against a ten year old girl, a butter-seller.
Jones returned, died in America.

The Latinus Stone

Here stands the Latinus stone,
not removed from Whithorn, it's stayed home.
Unlike most relics it hasn't gone
to an Edinburgh museum.
Debate continues over Latin translations,
though it's agreed to be evidence of congregations
of Christians, literacy, native Briton's sophistication.
Is it a funeral inscription or aristocratic donation?
Does the Latin word 'sinum' mean refuge or church?
They're scholarly questions but I don't care much.
I'm convinced of their value and intellectual fun
'Erected by Barradus a nephew or grandson
Of Latinus, thirty-five and his four year old daughter'.

The main puzzle is, where was the mother?

Alexander Murray: 1775–1813

A shepherd's son, born at Dunkitterick,
frail child unable to help on the moors.
But farming's loss was language's gain, his sick
disposition allowed learning indoors.

The Bible, Penny Ballads recited,
his pen stub of heather charcoal – a birn.
Abbyssinian, Arabic learned,
nine syllables are languages' foundations.

Leaving behind his Galloway village,
Edinburgh University beckoned-
Professor of Oriental languages.

But chronic ill-health hadn't been reckoned.
His translator's skills in Abbyssinian,
left his widow an eighty pound pension.

'No future age shall see his name expire'

Inscription on the tombstone of William Nicholson.

Brither Wull, tae scuil's routine ye wir ill-fitted,
they said ye could cairrie the pack insteid.
No suitit tae ferm wi yer short sicht,
loadit up wi combs, thimbles, goun fabric.
Ye set aff wi yer bagpipes at twentie,
wunnert whit wid printin a buik dae fir ye.

Afore lang yer poem sangs got ye kent,
tae Edinburgh citie neist ye went.
Bit doon in London ye fell oan herd times,
preachin religion instead o yer rhymes.
Drink made ye prey tae malevolent types.
Near droont in canals, robbed o yer pipes.

Ye'll be mindit alangside Burns an Hogg,
fir yer Brownie o Blednoch written at Borgue.

Memories of a Dumfriesshire Heroine

Born on a summer's day, Jane Haining,
at Lochenhead farm with siblings sharing
a Dumfries Academy education,
and rural childhood, gentle, caring.

Next, at eighteen to Glasgow city,
Domestic Science, St.Colm's Missionary,
alongside church work was more education.
In Budapest she found her calling.

Jane's last trip home, World War Two looming,
from Dunscore village, her sister was waving.
Pinning yellow stars on Jewish girls' clothing,
then Auschwitz prison, death by gassing.

A stained glass window in a Glasgow church
commemorates bravery, enduring much.

Merrick tae Criffel

*When a vehicle was needed for telling the terrible story of the
Foot and Mouth outbreak, in 2001, hills seemed appropriate;
they are very ancient, have an overview from high above the
population, and span the length of the region from East to West.
Here, two hills, in the south west of Scotland, speak to each
other. Merrick speaks in Scots and Criffel speaks in English.*

Criffel, ye're greetin!
Tell me o yer sadness.
Whit's wrang?

My eyes are misted, yes.
An acrid smoke burns here.

Why, whit's burnin there?
Hoo can it sclimb sae high
that you can see it fae yer
ain hill tap?

Pyres burn all round me
far as the eye can see.
Sheep have been lifted
from my foothills and slopes,
shot with guns, set alight
and buried in graves.

Criffel, I ken noo why
mists o tears are roon ye
A'd weep an aw if sic a
tragedy came westwards.

Cattle are being culled,
farms are devastated.
Around me strong men

are weeping. Also,
their children stay home.
Farm lanes and road ends are
sealed off, straw is soaked

in disinfectant and no
deliveries are made.
Few visitors arrive.
No-one leaves home much.

Oh Merrick, I hope your
green Galloway never
has to bear this darkness
I am thinking of the

old days, old names, past words.
They don't tell of the grim
reality of this.

'elf-shot' – listen and I'll

tell you of this old word.
The ailment in the beasts
was caused by fairies,
it's what it meant. Oh that

it were so, and
summoning fairies
was enough to stop the
spread of vileness through my

land, beseech them to lift
off their spell, charm us
back to happy days and
healthy beasts; wholesome hearts.

Aye, the aul wirds wir guid.
Thir wis *'croittich'* a lameness
an *'lung socht'*, disease,
an gin we seen a

broch aroon the muin
we kent puir times wid come
betides bad wather.
Aye, there maun be a broch aroon
the muin the nicht.

We are powerless to change this.
All we can do is wait and hope
for these farmers were struggling already
diversification was needed
some were trying.
Here's the tale of one:

For years he'd lifted stones,
tried to clear his land
of rubble, pulled out
hawthorn and gorse.

Now here's the son,
full of new ideas;
organic milk, ice-cream, yoghurt,
adventure playgrounds

Lay matting round the trees.
No chemicals needed
to kill weeds,
just large stones to weigh it down.

Full circle they'll come some day,
father and son united under
the family headstone,
moss gathering green,

wind whistling through the same trees.
All plans, people, laid to rest,
whaups circling above,
stones still lodged in the field's corner.

Like us, Criffel,
lodged in the region's corners,
we're seein doon the centuries
watchin, waitin,
an A've never seen the likes o this.

Not even through wars, Merrick
Independence,
Covenanters,
World Wars.

Sic a slauchter is a bleck merk
on wir souls.

Unless, like they say,
it was the only way?

* * *

Oh Criffel, it's came.
The blackness has travellt
tae ma green lans fillt wi
Beltit Galloways, Chambrolets, Ling.
Fires are blazin across the Machars.
The nicht lit wi reid an gowd
o burnin beasts. A mingin reek
fills awbodies thrapple an
greetin can be heard gin
the nicht gans quate.
A've never seen strang men cry, Criffel.
Even loast oan ma hills an a white haar
stoppin them fae finnin hame,
they didna sob sae.

But their beasts are their lives, Merrick.

Aye, even kennin fine that aw roads wid lead
tae slauchter onieweys –

but this is different, meaningless,
and even fine beasts for breeding
are cut down.

Wastin bonnie beasts
whyles hauf the warld starves oan.
It's no richt. Noo whit?
Criffel, A'm like an empty haun.

Ye ken ma name Merrick
is fae the Gaelic fir
a fork or branch – Meurach?
An Meur is a finnger,
an aw ma wee-er hills
rin doon like lang finngers
ablow me, Bennan an

Benyellary. Neist there's
Kirrieoch, Tarfessock
Shalloch an Minnock.
Aw o us thegither
in the palm o wir hills.
Hauns held sic prizes fir
kye, heichest haud yowes.

Oh Criffel, noo A'm
A tuim haun, lik
a mither whae's loss her
weans. Bairns she rearit
an fed, growed weel on ma
pastures rich, sweet coolin
burns tumblin throu ma glens –
Wigtown an Stewartry
Kirkcudbright – aw ma shires.

Merrick – now we will weep
together for we share
this tragedy, these deaths.
Grieve for our beasts, weep for

our farmers who worked long
and hard in every
season, lambing through snow,
calfing in sharp rain fall.

And now they talk of carriers.

Carriers?

Yes. Might the birds be bringing this
disease from afar?
The wintering geese carrying trouble?
If so, they say, we must cull them.

Never. We canna. We maunna.
Kill the birds fir fleein?
Greylag geese,
Greenlan white Fronts,
Baikals fae Russia,
Bewick's fae Finlan,
Whoopers fae Icelan,
Barnacles.
Oh, shairly we'll no hiv tae loss them?
The verra birds o the air
as weel as the beasts o the lan?

There's black times here, Merrick.
Close your eyes
and pray for a better morning.

We've seen sic sights
fae wir high vantage points:

A farmer at Ae still
goes out on his quad bike
with his sheep dogs
every day, same time,
though the fields are empty
of beasts.

The fermer at Auchlean
feeds his beasts thou
he kens fine they'll be killt
the morra
*'Ye widna lea them starvin
even thou'*, he tells ye.

A farmhouse window is coated
with grease, fat from the burning animals.

An naethin can be moved:

Away wintered sheep on the hills,

the store cattle needin tae move,

cast cows ready for slaughter –

an the fodder's rinnin low
soon the'll be nane

They burn with railway sleepers,
best grade coal
(too low is inefficient, the pyre
will burn for three weeks)

Bury deep, avoid water running below
seepage leads to contamination
one farmer and his wife
found blood seeping from a pipe.

Rats have arrived at some sites.
'Pigeons are flying rats'
Birkshaw Forest – a name etched
in our minds – mass gravesite.

A black faced gurkha
– strange sight at Sorbie,
the white suit shining against his skin,
six small children hiding by
the village hall watching,
as he closed the road, checked passing cars,
held his gun in readiness.
What did he hope for?
What will the children mind
of these times?

Aye bit they've taen aff
the soldiers o echteen year aul

a sad sight an open gate
– a sure sign all's gone

A wumman in Glasserton
liftit her cairpets
brung in her pet rams

Yin farmer said
it's an odd thing tae hear
yer ain voice echo in
a bull shed.

I heard whispers from Lammermuir
talking to Lothians,
and down to the Fells
where they're sick to their bones.

Aye, the Carricks were callin
tae Assynt aw nicht,
an Ailsa Craig let oot
a lang souch in the nicht.
Awbodie's worried seeck.

If only it wis aw by. A'll tell ye aboot ma dream.

As I gaed bi the Lunky Hole
A seen thir wir nae beasts
nae kye wir lowin ower green knowes
jist craws peckin feasts.

As I past bi the Lunky Hole
a kent the parks wir bare
nae yowes wir sprauchlin throu the gap
nae lambs joukin rare.

Oh wad we hae a Lunky Hole
whaur Time's driftin fair
the beasts aw fine, the lans sae fresh
an this Silent Spring nae mair.

But silence won't last.
Voices will be heard again.
Our fields dotted white
once more with sheep,
the baabaa chorus singing
next spring.
A fine farmer, resilient as ever says,
the'll be a bit remnant left.

Well, I hope he's right for
I've heard many a sad tale this year.
And I've heard angry ones too,
for now voices are being heard.

Aye, vyces wull be heard again
askin questions,
speirin o why guid beasts wir killt at aw?
speirin wis it aw fir the sake o siller?
speirin wis thir no anither wey?

A sacrifice maybe, all a sacrifice
to global markets, export, trade.
Maybe they just needed to
thin out a bit in the south?

For what does it matter in the
quiet south west?

Aye, wha bothers aboot us?
We're no even Munros, Criffel.
we dinna even catch the baggers.
Naethin tae shout aboot here,
even tho the braith is taen fae ye
gin ye drive thon Solway coast
past the shining, wet sands by Creetown.

Or the fine forest of Mabie
and the bonnie Sweetheart Abbey.
You're right, Merrick,
there's a lot more needing done
to tell the world of our secret south.

Aw Scotland's crammed intae
its middle.
Let yer belt oot, Caledonia,
cast yer een soothwards an aw.
Mind ye've Lowlands jist as green
as yer Hielans, an fine an mild tae stroll in.

A country garden, this region,
where the silent farmer waits in his home,
looking over the empty fields,
hoping for a new dawn.

Tenant Fermer
'We are the tenant fermers,
we dinna own these lans.
We are only rentin them
tae tend them wi wir hans.'

Land Owner
We are the owners
Of these farms and homes.
We lend a field to graze some sheep
Or let the cattle roam.

God
You are all tenant farmers.
I own the earth.
Your world is only borrowed
Till called to heaven's hearth.

Mither Natur
Naethin's owned bi onie o yes.
mind this or else.
Ilka cell, ilka livin thing,
is its ain self.
There is danger if ye forget.
Tak heed, manage wisely...
or fret.

Burning Whins

for Peter at Myrton

Here, where the soft grass rolls down to the loch
and the ruined castle dreams of a lost lifestyle,

we're far from strife. Far from the superpower plotting carnage,
or, the black horror which plucks small lives

from quiet family gatherings.
For the moment, we are blessed;

each visitor free to believe or not,
fortunate to count blessings if we wish.

On that first visit here, we set off on a tour
of the land, the lore, the legacy.

The disused chapel, now a store room,
where marriages, baptisms, funerals were held.

He can recall the last of them, points out the very window
of the room he was born in.

Returning from years in the city's buzz,
he's back to the garden which hosts loved ones' ashes,

sends up roses to scent friend's houses, to a Myrton
filled with farm folks' voices, family matters.

Crossing the fields, he sat in the pick-up truck
comfortable as an armchair, jumped out

to unlock gates, memories, stories,
name small lochans in the hill,

tell us of Mad Mary of Monreith
seeking justice and a house,

or, of the dead author of otters,
or, of Saint Medan's blinded beauty.

Once, women tied spring snowdrop bouquets,
when the walled garden's contents went to market.

Stopping high on the hill at whins,
he lit a match, held it to the dark, brittle branches.

The wind took it and the bush blazed,
yellower than the whins in bloom;

scene as ancient as a bible story.
Unsaid were the words,

This is our land.
Here is my home.
These are my roots.

And I, landless, root shifting,
marvelled at such ownership,
that allows a man to burn whins

Two Wanlockhead poems

1. Touch the Lucky Lead

If only it was so easy
but fate's sealed the future.

No fortune's found
at a forefinger's touch;
the spot rubbed clean,
lead shining silver,
on cold cave walls.

Transforming base materials,
it's what we all want;
lives altered to perfection overnight,
when really we work away silently,
long term,

rubbing till we've fashioned
an existence into
something manageable,

sometime striking gold.

*Note: At Wanlockhead mining village, the miners would rub a
patch on the wall at the entrance to the cave, in the hope that
they would not be involved in an accident and that they might
find precious metals.*

2. Fern

Here, deep in a cave dark,
lacking air, a fern grows.

Fed by the smallest drip
seeping from lead slate

it's flourished.
See its glossy leaves shine.

Watch the water caught
in the camera's quick lens,

green fronds outstretched like palms.

That life can spore
and grow in such frail light!

Celebrate the shadows,
for fresh starts can fall out of them.

Around us, unseen,
nothing need be truly lost.

Slowly, much is possible,
even from darkness.

Note: Deep in an old mining cave, a tiny drip of water has been enough to allow a fern to grow.

Walking Glen Trool

There is nothing like
the wind on your face.

You cannot feel it in a prison
or in a hospital,

Neither can you feel it in a cave
looking at spiders.

There is nothing like
the wind in your face.

You cannot feel it when
your mind is locked in sadness

or your heart is broken.
Neither can you feel it when

your senses are dulled by pain
or the corpse lies still in its coffin.

Here, sitting with you,
on the shores of this still loch,

young spring trees greening around us,
and our old love seasoning so well,

we know our good fortune;
feel the wind on our faces.

The Whithorn Lecture

Resurgam: I shall rise again (Whithorn Motto)

For lo, the winter is past,
the rain is over and done.
the flowers appear on the earth;
the time of the singing of birds is come.
The figtree puts forth her green figs,
and the wine with the tender grape give a good smell.
from The Song of Solomon
quoted in Daphne Brooke's 'Wild Men and Holy Places.'

Delivered annually, it's well kent,
dated in diaries a year hence.
This Saturday evening, folk travel from afar
to hear learned words.

Driving through dusk,
the September night is dark fields;
headlights startle animal eyes,
small creatures scurry across beams.

Dead hedgehogs, rabbits, foxes litter the road –
detritus of every country lane in every Scottish town.

To the North, neon blinks, discos tune up.
cities busy up for Saturday night's buzz.

They have risen again.

Here, in the wide market square,
cars arrive, disgorge passengers,
in tweed, corduroy, woollen jumpers.

Street-strolling teenagers chew gum,
hands in pockets, cropped hair, nylon jackets.
They glance at visitors, shout comments,
proceed down cobbled streets.

From the Priory, their cries can still be heard
sharp words echoing from the open length of road.

Shut shops on either side absorb nothing.
Sweet papers blow into corners, lodge glued by stickiness.

Resurgam: I shall rise again.

In the Priory the audience settle.
Collective ages stretch to infinity,
the lecturer adds her own eight decades.

Frail, in a wheelchair the strong voice
belies her frame, and finds its way to
every nook and cranny of the silent church

Stone walls, stained glass, oak pews
perfect backdrop for the script.
Pre-Christianity is this year's theme.

She tells of Celtic goddesses, pagan shrines
overturned as Christian men convert the locals.
These incomers said they knew a better way to live.

Ancient vandalism displayed as standing stones
become recumbent and KYROS replace
cups and rings. No Celtic goddess then would meet you
at the sacred well.

Resurgam: I shall rise again.

This town has lived through change.
Once a place of pilgrimage, visited by Kings,
blessed by votive-seeking saints,

a vital harbour link in days when ships were all
and sea-faring folk made the town
a first class port of call.

Bartering voices cried of
African glass phials,
Mediterranean silver,
fine Phoenician pots.

Before the road was king
and Whithorn still looked seaward,
proudly welcomed trade
with worldwide lands.

Now, in this landlocked century,
terrain vast, journeys slow,
south-west towns relegated
to small town status,
sea tragedies still cut
and beasts have burnt here.

Resurgam: I shall rise again.

City saints like Mungo were such louder lads than
Ninian, Nynia, Ringan, Trinian,
whose softly, softly prints were kept a quiet secret
in Physgill's cave as the sea sprayed sounds.
Columba gets the kudos for Christianity coming.

The lecturer's voice grows fainter, she must rest.
The audience clap, rise to leave, move to cars.

Outside, the boys in dark jackets
still tramp the market town's streets.
Lodge firm like crisp packets piling at doorways,
wait for a wind gust strong enough to make a difference.

The century turns again. A Parliament returns;
its stated aim democracy, decentralisation.
Which way will the wind blow now?

Resurgam. I shall rise again

*This poem formed part of a choral recitation entitled 'Timeless'
and was performed by The Feral Choir.*

SECTION III
Picasso's Timeshare

'art is a lie that allows us to approach the truth', Picasso.

Picasso's Timeshare

1.

In his allotted timespan –
eighty two years –

dwelling in a Europe
troubled by strife;

world, civil, domestic;
more than his fair

share of disharmony,
but also love,

this twentieth century icon
weathered the elements

in Spain and France;
viewed earth from all sides cubist fashion,

stunning a turbulent world,
with his work.

Here, at this Spanish timeshare in his birth town,
I'm giving him a week;

a time when twenty-first century Europe
accedes new nations to its union;

but another Middle Eastern country
verges on civil war;

a time when famine and drought
still plague half our world

but more millionaires are made
every month.

At Pablo Ruiz Picasso airport,
I touch down from a sky brushed with cheap flights;

strain for a glimpse of his '*White Dove of Peace*'.

2.

Picasso said,

'*the day will come when all men
will be able to live like the rich and powerful
of former times, surrounded, in short, by beauty*'.

Siesta fades into dusk, into night.
The grass cutter has stopped his drone,
having swathed his way through the day,
field strimmed, and Spanish trees
tall, neat, trim; merging manicured into

the Timeshare mould.
Another gardener dark, silent,
climbs into balconies to pluck
half-dead geraniums from dry soil.
Nature is pre-empted here,

groomed before decay sets in.
From the Aesthetic Clinic,
Gucci women, Versace men
follow the geranium route;
halt the march of death.

By the week's end, here where
poverty means not affording
the face lift till next year,
I've seen few old folk.
Picasso might have been at home.

A biography informs me
of all the women he had:
Marie-Therese,
Francoise, Jacqueline,
the list is endless.
Still, it's the black clothed widows
in the nearbye village,
wrinkled old fishermen at the Port
that I recall.

3.

*There is a story of Abetz looking
at a reproduction of 'Guernica' and asking:
'Did you do that, Monsieur Picasso?'
To which Picasso replied: 'No, you did!'*

Art being the product
of its time,
the artist a medium
through which
pictures come,
or words flourish.

We've had,
the unmade bed,
formaldehyde sheep,
concepts becoming central.

Sharing time,
we strive in our own centuries,
to depict the present,
impose order over chaos.

4.

Picasso said:
You never paint the Parthenon;
you never paint a Louis XV armchair.
You make pictures out of some little house in the Midi,
a packet of tobacco, or an old chair.

It is in the smallest of everyday matters
we find our art;
poetry from the woman next door,
lyrics from the supermarket's labels,
songs from a baby's mouth.

Striving for the greatest things;
bigger pictures,
the road is small and local.

Amongst the chickens
and red wheelbarrows,
our days lived out,
our dreams elsewhere.

5.

Picasso said
on Cubists:

The appearance of a subject from one point of view was insufficient.
It should be conceived from all angles.
They painted what they knew to be there.

We could do with a bit of the old Cubism here, eh Pablo?
Especially after Madrid's suicide bombers.
Able to see all sides, back, front, behind,
what's in a backpack.
Not just what's in sight.
Hola!
Please open your bags, Senora.
Let the cat out of it.

6.

Picasso said,
at Vallauris, village of potters.

Show me that man, always so gentle
who claimed that the fingers make the earth rise,
 (for Andrew)

You aren't a potter
though you might have been.
Instead, raw sandstone, ungiving granite
your medium, as you
mosaic a trail of beauty
in many gardens.

You dug in Highland soil in your early days;
northern gales never stopped your play;
frozen Moray Firth never stopped you paddling;
your gentle nature soft beside stone
one with your elements of choice.

Your hands making the earth rise;
occasionally, hearts soar.

7.

Picasso said,
Everything you can imagine is real.

Purchases at the Timeshare

For fifteen hundred Euros, you can have
eyeball jewellery, implants.

A fifteen minute operation will insert a
three point five millimeter piece,

of specially developed jewellery, into
the eye's mucous membrane.

A glittering half-moon
and a heart are available.

Jewels only visible when
the eye is turned.

A waiting list already exists.

A glossy mag explains how
you can clone your pet.

Folk have phoned in.
'I have a ball my dog played with.

It's covered with saliva.
Can you clone from that?

Or a bit of fur?
A tooth?'

Unfortunately, a couple of months
is too late.

Only within a few days of death
can the procedure be done.

Start to think of it now,
a swatch from your dog's stomach,

your beloved cat's inner mouth.
And start saving,

the fifty thousand dollars,
so you're ready.

8.

Picasso said,
to his father,
Leave me your brushes, your cane,
or give me the little pigeon.

Not wanting to cross
the school threshold,

Picasso pled for these things;
deposits to ensure his father's return.

Scottish in the fifties,
there were no such things to ask for.

Mothers carried no pigeons,
just brothers and sisters.

No art was created by fathers,
maybe gardens if they grew them at all.
A cane not a prop for an old man,
but a Calvinist's control tool.

No hot Spanish blood
filling our cold young veins.

9.

Picasso said,
of his own poetry,
Painted in words, with lines taut as harpstrings.

Mair lik a bugle it seems, ma shout,
no findin the harpstring's voice.

Mair, a jiggin fiddle cries
Aye an hoochaye ower

islands, bens, lochs, or,

the soun o silence,
oan an empty raised beach.

An, lacking his multi-skills,
the canvas no covered.

Sometimes he even paintit wi feathers,
insteid o brushes.

Picked fae his flair,
drapt by his pigeons.

No even a quill, shapit an pointit,
an us inkin anither art form

fae words an souns,
wantin his tautness.

10.

Sabartes said,
There was, 'A time when the Catalan language
quivered like a flag in the breeze'.

Oor kintra too, has seen sic times,
  saltire shoogly in a nordern gale,
     blawin oor words aff doon a suddren
   coast.
  Noo, we're ettlin fir a strang spell,
the wind ayeweys ahint us.

11.

Poussin said,
You must realize that there are two ways of seeing an object,
one by casually looking, the other by studying it
with close attention.

The orange seen entire,
or,
dissected into segments.

The poem seen whole,
or,
segmented by discussion.

The taste of each,
sweet in your hands, if long enough
to ripen in the sun.

12.

Picasso said,
*The artist must discover a way to convince the general public
of the complete truth of his lies.*

I'm reading of
trompe l'oeil: something pretending to be something else.

More like the wool has been pulled
over ours in the superpower's invasion,

to find weapons of mass destruction,
rid a nation of a dictator.

Perhaps oil *will* flow freely,
But, if profits are shared unequally,

we'll see it for what it was:
the perfect trompe l'oeil.

13.

Picasso said,
Each picture is a phial filled with my blood.
That is what has gone into it.

A matador might have said the same,
his lifeblood pouring over a bull ring floor.

The artist, meanwhile, channelling
violent thoughts onto canvas.

Such commitment from both.
The heart might sink,

ink not doing the same job,
not enough shed onto paper.

Some of us lead such ordinary lives,
even tear drops a scarcity,

little in a cosy life needing sacrifice,
devotion to causes,

Martyrdom;
commitments that can kill,

though we empty
our pens onto paper,

with the histories of others.

SECTION IV
Found objects

'What comes out in the end is the result of discarded finds'
Picasso

found object

inside my sugar puffs
this morning
was an alien

pink and rubbery
a translucent jelly
good enough to eat

I wondered who it
 was modelled on
And was there somewhere

far away on a distant planet
an antennaed gastropod
opening his galactic cornflakes

to find a small
flesh coloured woman
in need of a good

dusting down?

Dusk

Mahonia, it is, but
you can't recall my plant's name,
barely see it with your
eighty year old eyes,
forgetting how to focus.

Yet once a gardener,
a Park's Department worker,
you knew the names of every plant, like
the back of my hand, which you held,
then filled with ox-eye daisies, chrysants.

Eagle-eyed, you'd
tour the glass houses,
supervise the spring beds going in,
close the Park at Dusk as the sign said.

This, I remember,
disturbed me.
When is Dusk, I'd ask.
When the dark comes, you said.
Late in summer,
early in winter.

The memory now surfaces,
as we stop you stumbling,
on the garden path.
Tell you again, *It's Mahonia,*
not knowing when
Dusk might fall.

Everything had been washed

Everything had been washed
for it had rained all night.
Good housewives
hung out clean sheets
on lines taught
like tethered ghosts.

The white fabric flaps.
No signs or stains
remain of past events,
shady liaisons,
haemorràging of dreams,
for everything had been washed.

If it could happen;
a brainwash,
flushing out fights,
bite-your-tongue barneys,
tit-for-tat flyting,
swear words,
soaked through,
rinsed, lost in
a last good spin
like this sweet smelling,
virgin-like curtain,
opening and closing
when hands unclasp
restraining pegs and,
all is back at the start again,
ready to begin again,
for everything had been washed.

Yet here is the rain,
the gale, the storm,
the bird shit accompanying
shrieking from gulls flying
sudden.

You can never be sure when
the weather will turn.
Each day rise in hope,
start afresh, cleanse,
stand back, wait,
watch the beauty
of the flapping
in the wind
of the clean white sheets,
happy souls, for
everything had been washed.

Clausemetric surgery

A fresh poem
eyes me from the page.
Like a patient under operation,
it's for the chop,
and it knows it.

A liposuction job,
it has to shed a bit.
Nips and tucks
make all the difference.
Small sounds litter the margin
                              like tears.

But, after a while,
lying
          low,
unseen,
convalescing,
it'll thank me for it
when
a trim, lean shape,
not a stanza spare or excess syllable
lies   spread   out
between clean white sheets.

Off-sales

Today, in Vicki Wine,
I was buying booze,
all bottles, no cans.

An assistant said sharply,
goods in her hand,
There's a problem, this doesn't scan.

Startled from my musings,
(queues are good for
dreaming over poems),

I wondered how she knew,
it was a free verse piece
I mulled on?

The till flashed fiercely,
waiting for a bar code entry.
I twigged at last.

But, damage done,
I'd lost the muse.
Pledged, in future,

to choose my shops,
and words,
more carefully.

The flight out

For us Brits, these quirky foreign practices can be often rather baffling.
(quote from 'In flight' magazine)

It's rude,

In Thailand:
to cross your legs in company
or point your toes at another person.

In Greece:
to show the palm of your hand while driving.

In Japan:
to maintain eye contact during conversation.

However,
it is illegal in:
California:
for women to drive in a housecoat.

In Texas:
to shoot a buffalo from the second storey of a hotel

In Alabama:
to wear a fake moustache that causes laughter in a church.

In Connecticut:
to educate a dog.

Ohio:
to get a fish drunk.

So now you know.
You have been warned.

Student
(for Jenny)

At the street of the flats,under
Autumn's confetti carpets,there's
no Parking Space left.

The road's full of Freshers,
parents, for a first University term.

Cars disgorge boxes of books,
kettles, toasters, cooking utensils,
computers, even televisions,

(things have changed since my days here)
Teenage kids supervise manouevres.

Behind every cardboard box,
a pale-faced parent stumbles.
It's reminiscent of first school days,

roles reversed,
as the school bell rang.

Now, kids walk briskly,
empty cars at speed,run up flights of stairs,
emphasise our growing slowness.

Does no one live on ground floors?
Like some mourner at a wake,

I'm following behind, funeral time,
arms weighted by dishes
for meals I'll no longer make her.

Years of being needed vanish
with every step up this tall, tenement flat.

For every stair I count the years, hear
the key turn in her new lock.
The cliche's wrong.

One door shuts as another door shuts.
I'm learning lives, unlike locks, can't be copied.

Heading off for A four paper, pens, folders,
preparations for the student's new day.
I wait, purse-at-the-ready,

watch her small figure dart between shelves,
and I'm searching too.

A Big Issue

Hey you Jimmy!
Aye you.
Gonnie gie us wan
o thae newspapers
unner yer airm
Much is it?
Whit?
A pun?
Gey dear.
Wait ti A see
whit A've goat
in ma pocket.
Forty pee, fifty pee
Here, whit's it caed?
'The Big Issue'?
Whit's that when it's at hame?
A newspaper fir the hameless?
Bit A've goat a hame.
Whit you huvnae?
How no?
Ye lost it?
How can ye loss yer hoose?
Here answer me.
A askt ye a question.
Pure dead ignorant, so ye ur.
A'm jist wantin a newsy
Want tae read aboot real issues
Things that's happenin in the real world
Folk starvin, bombs goin aff, murders
A care, ye ken. A care aboot folk.
Wisen up, man
Away an get real.

The Bard

Barred.
Dae ye ken that wurd?
Barred?
It widnae be the furst time
that wan o ma boys wis barred.
They're ayeweys getting barred
fae thir local.

Bit barred? Rabbie Burns,
oor National barred?
The telly said it.
It's aye fu o it in January.
Like a fifty nine bus ye ken,
nuthing fur ages then ye
cannae get movin fir them.

A huvtae admit A don't really
listen tae it aw. A hid enough
aw thae year ago at the scuil.
Bit they're still
bangin oan aboot Burns.
Ye'd of thought they'd of fun
anither wan bi noo.
A modrin wan.
Mibbe there isnae any.

Tae be honest, A blame the education system.
There's too much o it nooadays,
an A don't think Rabbie had any
an look whit it did fir him.

Bit it gied ye a laugh, thae poems.
We couldnae make heid nor tail o them,
bit we learnt them fir a wee man
wi a bald heid an a broon suit.

He'd come tae judge us,
fae the Federation, wid ye believe.
Well done, he wid say, *an excellent delivery.*
An gie us a book.

A mind rinnin hame wi it
an ma mammy said, *Weel din, hen,*
Let yer Auntie Nelly hear yer poem.
An A'd say it aw then,
Can A gan oot noo, Mammy?

An she said tae ma Auntie,
That weans language disnae get
Onie better, does it?

So, that's yer barred fir ye.
We used tae git barred fae gan oot.
Nooadays ye'd cry it grounded,
would ye no?

Ye huv tae keep up language wise.
As Burns himself said,
The times they are a-changin.
A hink.

A Guid Hing Fae Calton Hill

Huv ye ever hid a guid hing?
Dae ye ken whit a guid hing is?
Weel,ye fling open yer windae,
plant yer eblows ower the ledge,
an hae a guid gowp oot.

Sometimes ye hae a wee keek furst,
an somethin catches yer eye,ken,
a guid fecht or a wean gettin battered,
an ye want tae hae a better gowk.
Ye need tae mind yer rollers but,

they aye catch oan the windae frame.
A like tae hae ma rollers in-jist in case.
The guid thing aboot a guid hing is,
ye can see whit's cumin up yer close, be prepared n that.
Like thae thievin salesmen-ye see them cumin.

'Missus,would you be interested in a set of encyclopedias?
Answers to all your questions?'
Answers tae aw ma questions?Who's he kiddin?
A'll no get answers fae a big fat book.
Mind A could get them fae thon wee fat cooncillor,

bit he only cums oot in May.
Naw, A widnae tak ma rollers oot fur him.
Bit don't start me wi thae politics.
Did ye hear aboot aw thae fowk stood up Calton Hill?
A wheen o fowk fae aw the pairts

o 'Cool Caledonia' as they cried it.
Walked fae aw ower the place,
tae build a wee cairn up the hill-richt up the tap.
A wee hing fae Scotland, like me at ma windae,
only they wur lookin doon on some

o thae sleekit weys at Westminster.
Scunnert they ur. Cannae say A blame them.
Of course ye want tae keep yer ain schuils,
yer hospitals, yer railways. An watter-whit next?
A could fill a bucket on ma ain windae sill.

It's wur watter. See the mair ye think aboot it.

See if that wis me? A'd take a guid hing fur the last time-
Nae violence mind bit A'd jist slam ma windae shut
an hae nae mair tae dae wi them
till they came roon tae ma weys o thinkin.

Enough's enough A say.
Excuse the aggression. A've aye been like this
an A didnae take that fae the wind.
A bit o the auld Pict in me yet eh?
A'll away an get ma rollers oot

A've a feeling in ma bones
that somethins roon the corner.
Or am A jist kiddin masel again?

Sang o Bernadette
(for Mum)

At ma tenth birthday ma Ma surprist me,

A'm takin ye tae the Picters.
Spirits soared, the Picters wis wan thing,
mum tae masel wis anither.

Post-war Pathe News cracklt
lik soor ploom sweetie pokes.
Mum an me lik twa pals.

'The Song of Bernadette',
A wee lassie that becomes a saint.
Seein Mary at a grotto she fun

she cuid work miracles.
Her faimilie praised her, neibours flockt,
priests gaithert tae hear her blessin.

That faur fae a Glesca wean's life:
black sannies in summer, black wellies in winter.
Places o worship, the Church, Parkheid.

An noo ye swore ye'd be a nun,
Inhale sweet incense, stroke rosaries,
walk wi a saint's walk, barefit throu convents.

Next, yer Confirmation; bride-white dress,
real shoes. A jowl-slappin Bishop fills ye
wi holy Spirit.

Smeddum ye'd need much later,
tae say ye'd given up that Faith,
the sang lang deid in yer thrapple

Kosovo Sound Waves

On the radio,
an Irish journalist
was talking of Kosovo.

Over there, researching,
she'd met a woman who'd lost
four children in a café-bar massacre.

She talks of the sound,
of a dying child. A small phew.
The sound of your child dying.

The sound no-one wants to hear.
My own pale comparison,
years back, a six month foetus

stopped breathing.
Ultra sound thudded no heart beat,
only a dull machine whirr.

Three healthy children later,
I weep for this Kosovan mother,
running across towns,

desperate for shelter.
huddling in a cafe bar,
grenades and bullets follow.

Stench of burning flesh mingling
with coffee shop aromas.
Formica tables no barrier.

The Irish journalist herself is
no stranger to violence.
Her own nation familiar with

the dying child's sound.

Circling this globe, weeping women
have tears enough to weave a flood,
drown out every sound on earth.

On the radio
an Irish journalist
tried talking of Kosovo.

Thin Line

There's a man
walking the street
with his kettle.

It's the only way
he can be sure
he hasn't left it on.

A nurse comes
once a week and
shows him how

to shut his door and
walk away
not checking thirty times.

Who ever showed you
how to switch a kettle off?
Or shut a door only once?

How often have you
jumped the cracks
in the pavement?

Have you noticed
the
thin
line
between?

Midwinter blues

A colander of stars
is cupping us tonight.

Frosted pavements sparkle
with ones that have

fallen through.

My pockets are empty of stars
though I've reached for them often.

Between cracks in this
crystal pavement lie

all the poems I've never penned,
books I've never written.

December marches us
down the nights, to

the midwinter moment,
when time will turn into

tangerines falling through
too-big holes in a mesh bag.

Dreams will pass then too.

So many winters now,
you'd think you'd got their measure.

Like stars or poems,
they'll choose when or why,

or even if at all;
leave you alone as

thin pink streaks
herald morning.

When poetry is not enough
(for Christopher)

My wee nephew wants a story.
Tucked up under his Spiderman quilt he's waiting.
Posters on the wall watch us;
Superman, Batman, 007.

I want a made-up story not from a book, he adds.
My hearts sinks. My imagination's threatened.
I know it's a bonding opportunity but
I can't semi-sleep then, rote read while dozing.

Besides, that white wine waiting downstairs won't stay chilled.
Can it be about Ghengis Khan and William Wallace?
He compounds the complexity.
School history has a lot to answer for.

How is chronology handled for eight year olds?
Time-travel it'll have to be then. And I have been to Mongolia,
can describe the coloured flags welcoming warriors,
flapping in the desert's night breeze,

cream yurts glowing,
painted horses trapped forever circling the tented ceilings,
mane to tail like some Grecian vase folk.
My tale's not appreciated.

Just as I move onto William Wallace, heather covered hills,
his Mel Gibson-like stature and good looks,
my nephew interrupts, *What happens next?*
Fine turns of phrase, graphic descriptions are not needed,

he wants action, Hollywood style.
The poet in me wants to keep with the landscape,
move on to examine diverse cultures,
East, West, Christian, Muslim,

I'm left looking at his wee face,
white as the moon lurking past his star patterened curtains.
I'm stymied, outside my comfort zone,
asking with him, *What happens next?*

Some other books published by **LUATH** PRESS

POETRY

Drink the Green Fairy
Brian Whittingham
ISBN 1 84282 020 6 PB £8.99

Tartan & Turban
Bashabi Fraser
ISBN 1 84282 044 3 PB £8.99

The Ruba'iyat of Omar Khayyam, in Scots
Rab Wilson
ISBN 1 84282 046 X PB £8.99

Talking with Tongues
Brian D. Finch
ISBN 1 84282 006 0 PB £8.99

Kate o Shanter's Tale and other poems [book]
Matthew Fitt
ISBN 1 84282 028 1 PB £6.99

Kate o Shanter's Tale and other poems [audio CD]
Matthew Fitt
ISBN 1 84282 043 5 PB £9.99

Bad Ass Raindrop
Kokumo Rocks
ISBN 1 84282 018 4 PB £6.99

Madame Fifi's Farewell and other poems
Gerry Cambridge
ISBN 1 84282 005 2 PB £8.99

Poems to be Read Aloud
introduced by Tom Atkinson
ISBN 0 946487 00 6 PB £5.00

Scots Poems to be Read Aloud
introduced by Stuart McHardy
ISBN 0 946487 81 2 PB £5.00

Picking Brambles
Des Dillon
ISBN 1 84282 021 4 PB £6.99

Sex, Death & Football
Alistair Findlay
ISBN 1 84282 022 2 PB £6.99

The Luath Burns Companion
John Cairney
ISBN 1 84282 000 1 PB £10.00

Immortal Memories: A Compilation of Toasts to the Memory of Burns as delivered at Burns Suppers, 1801-2001
John Cairney
ISBN 1 84282 009 5 HB £20.00

The Whisky Muse: Scotch whisky in poem & song
Robin Laing
ISBN 1 84282 041 9 PB £7.99

A Long Stride Shortens the Road
Donald Smith
ISBN 1 84282 073 7 PB £8.99

Into the Blue Wavelengths
Roderick Watson
ISBN 1 84282 075 3 PB £8.99

FICTION

Torch
Lin Anderson
ISBN 1 84282 042 7 PB £9.99

Heartland
John MacKay
ISBN 1 84282 059 1 PB £9.99

The Blue Moon Book
Anne MacLeod
ISBN 1 84282 061 3 PB £9.99

The Glasgow Dragon
Des Dillon
ISBN 1 84282 056 7 PB £9.99

Driftnet
Lin Anderson
ISBN 1 84282 034 6 PB £9.99

The Fundamentals of New Caledonia
David Nicol
ISBN 1 84282 93 6 HB £16.99

Milk Treading
Nick Smith
ISBN 1 84282 037 0 PB £6.99

The Road Dance
John MacKay
ISBN 1 84282 024 9 PB £6.99

The Strange Case of RL Stevenson
Richard Woodhead
ISBN 0 946487 86 3 HB £16.99

But n Ben A-Go-Go
Matthew Fitt
ISBN 0 946487 82 0 HB £10.99
ISBN 1 84282 014 1 PB £6.99

The Bannockburn Years
William Scott
ISBN 0 946487 34 0 PB £7.95

Outlandish Affairs: An Anthology of Amorous Encounters
Edited and introduced by Evan Rosenthal and Amanda Robinson
ISBN 1 84282 055 9 PB £9.99

FOLKLORE

Scotland: Myth Legend & Folklore
Stuart McHardy
ISBN 0 946487 69 3 PB £7.99

The Supernatural Highlands
Francis Thompson
ISBN 0 946487 31 6 PB £8.99

Tall Tales from an Island
Peter Macnab
ISBN 0 946487 07 3 PB £8.99

Tales from the North Coast
Alan Temperley
ISBN 0 946487 18 9 PB £8.99

THE QUEST FOR

The Quest for Robert Louis Stevenson
John Cairney
ISBN 0 946487 87 1 HB £16.99

The Quest for the Nine Maidens
Stuart McHardy
ISBN 0 946487 66 9 HB £16.99

The Quest for the Original Horse Whisperers
Russell Lyon
ISBN 1 842820 020 6 HB £16.99

The Quest for the Celtic Key
Karen Ralls-MacLeod and Ian Robertson
ISBN 1 842820 031 1 PB £8.99

The Quest for Arthur
Stuart McHardy
ISBN 1 842820 12 5 HB £16.99

The Quest for Charles Rennie Mackintosh
John Cairney
ISBN 1 84282 058 3 HB £16.99

ON THE TRAIL OF

On the Trail of John Muir
Cherry Good
ISBN 0 946487 62 6 PB £7.99

On the Trail of Mary Queen of Scots
J. Keith Cheetham
ISBN 0 946487 50 2 PB £7.99

On the Trail of William Wallace
David R. Ross
ISBN 0 946487 47 2 PB £7.99

On the Trail of Robert Burns
John Cairney
ISBN 0 946487 51 0 PB £7.99

On the Trail of Bonnie Prince Charlie
David R. Ross
ISBN 0 946487 68 5 PB £7.99

On the Trail of Queen Victoria in the Highlands
Ian R. Mitchell
ISBN 0 946487 79 0 PB £7.99

On the Trail of Robert the Bruce
David R. Ross
ISBN 0 946487 52 9 PB £7.99

On the Trail of Robert Service
GW Lockhart
ISBN 0 946487 24 3 PB £7.99

LANGUAGE

Luath Scots Language Learner [Book]
L Colin Wilson
ISBN 0 946487 91 X PB £9.99

Luath Scots Language Learner [Double Audio CD Set]
L Colin Wilson
ISBN 1 84282 026 5 CD £16.99

WALK WITH LUATH

Mountain Days & Bothy Nights
Dave Brown and Ian Mitchell
ISBN 0 946487 15 4 PB £7.50

The Joy of Hillwalking
Ralph Storer
ISBN 1 84282 069 9 PB £7.50

Scotland's Mountains before the Mountaineers
Ian R. Mitchell
ISBN 0 946487 39 1 PB £9.99

Mountain Outlaw
Ian R. Mitchell
ISBN 1 84282 027 3 PB £6.50

Luath Press Limited
committed to publishing well written books worth reading

LUATH PRESS takes its name from Robert Burns, whose little collie Luath (*Gael.*, swift or nimble) tripped up Jean Armour at a wedding and gave him the chance to speak to the woman who was to be his wife and the abiding love of his life. Burns called one of *The Twa Dogs* Luath after Cuchullin's hunting dog in *Ossian's Fingal*. Luath Press was established in 1981 in the heart of Burns country, and is now based a few steps up the road from Burns' first lodgings on Edinburgh's Royal Mile. Luath offers you distinctive writing with a hint of unexpected pleasures.

Most bookshops in the UK, the US, Canada, Australia, New Zealand and parts of Europe either carry our books in stock or can order them for you. To order direct from us, please send a £sterling cheque, postal order, international money order or your credit card details (number, address of cardholder and expiry date) to us at the address below. Please add post and packing as follows: UK – £1.00 per delivery address; overseas surface mail – £2.50 per delivery address; overseas airmail – £3.50 for the first book to each delivery address, plus £1.00 for each additional book by airmail to the same address. If your order is a gift, we will happily enclose your card or message at no extra charge.

Luath Press Limited
543/2 Castlehill
The Royal Mile
Edinburgh EH1 2ND
Scotland
Telephone: 0131 225 4326 (24 hours)
Fax: 0131 225 4324
email: gavin.macdougall@luath.co.uk
Website: www.luath.co.uk